How do I know the course is **right for me**?

- ☐ Are you a parent or carer of one or more children aged 11 to 18 years old?

- ☐ Would you like to meet other parents at a similar stage?

- ☐ Would you like your family life to be the best it can be?

- ☐ Are you struggling as a parent of a teenager?

- ☐ Would you like to improve your skills as a parent of this age group?

If you answered 'yes' to any of those questions then this course is for you, whether you feel all is going well or you are facing challenges.

While The Parenting Teenagers Course is based on Christian principles, it is designed for parents and carers with or without a Christian faith.

The course is for every type of parenting situation, including parenting on your own, step-parenting and parenting as a couple.

Whatever your situation, the practical tools you learn can help to improve and strengthen your family life.

What is The Parenting Teenagers Course?

The Parenting Teenagers Course was developed by Nicky and Sila Lee, authors of *The Marriage Book* and *The Parenting Book*. They have been married for over thirty years, have four children and live in London. They started The Parenting Teenagers Course in 1997, and it continues to spread with many courses now running around the world.

Over five sessions (or ten shorter ones) you will discover practical tools to help you:

- **Keep** your long-term aim in mind
- **Meet** your teenagers' needs
- **Set** effective boundaries
- **Help** develop your teenagers' emotional health
- **Pass** on values and help them make good choices

What can I **expect** on the course?

A great atmosphere
that is welcoming, encouraging and fun. Courses are run in all kinds of venues – homes, restaurants, cafes (after hours), community halls, churches, schools – but wherever your local course is run, you should find a great atmosphere and a friendly welcome.

A delicious meal or snack
– each session begins with something to eat and drink, giving you space to relax and chat to other parents/carers.

Practical talks
that are informative and fun, either given live or played on DVD. They include filmed clips of parents and teenagers sharing their own experiences, street interviews and advice from parenting experts.

Small groups based on the age of your oldest child
so that you can meet other parents/carers who are at a similar stage to you.

Time to discuss
the challenges you are facing and how to establish long-term strategies for your own family. However, you will not be required to share anything about your family life that you would prefer not to. Every part of the course is optional, including contributing to the small group discussions.

What is the **cost** of the course?

Most courses charge a minimal fee to cover the cost of the meal, course materials and venue (if applicable). Your local course administrator will be able to let you know how much you'll need to pay. Many courses also offer bursaries.

What do **others say** about it?

> Don't just take our word for it – this is what past guests have said about the course

'**All the sessions tackle really good stuff, and they don't skirt around the issues**.'

'Hearing other parents is reassuring, and finding the tools to use is brilliant.'

'The course gave really helpful ways of dealing with seemingly impossible situations.'

'We've been given the tools to communicate better with our teenagers.'

'The course has broadened our minds ... big time!'

'It was very, very useful.'